CAT FLAPS!

NORTHERN MYSTERY CATS

ANDY ROBERTS

WITH A FOREWORD BY RICHARD FREEMAN

Edited by Jonathan Downes
Cover and internal design by Mark North for CFZ Communications
Using Microsoft Word 2000, Microsoft , Publisher 2000, Adobe Photoshop CS.
Unless otherwise stated all photographs are © Andy Roberts and
artwork is © Iain Johnstone.
First Edition published in 1986 by Brigantia Books, Brighouse, England
Revised and reprinted 1987
Reprinted 1992
Second Edition published in 2001 by CFZ
Third Edition published in 2007 by CFZ Press
CFZ Press
Myrtle Cottage
Woolfardisworthy
Bideford
North Devon
EX39 5QR

CFZ PRESS

© CFZ MMVII

ISBN: 978-1-905723-11-9

CONTENTS

RICHARD FREEMAN

FOREWORD

by Richard Freeman

Until recently a nocturnal ramble in British woodlands would be an un-thrilling affair. This little island has lost all its naturally occurring large predators. The wolverine was driven to extinction perhaps as far back as the last ice age. The brown bear bit the dust around 800 years ago. The wolf lingered on in the wilder areas for around another 400 years.

All this seems now to have changed. For decades there have been reports of huge powerful killers stalking our countryside. Creatures alien to the British environment that have, in some parts of the country, cut a bloody swathe through domestic livestock. We give these animals dramatic names such as the `Beast of Bodmin` or the `Beast of Exmoor`, transforming them into bloody fanged monsters.It is thrilling to think of creatures quite capable of killing a man once more abroad in our increasingly less green and pleasant land.

In reality they appear, in the main, to be specimens of the puma *(Puma concolor)* of the Americas and melanistic forms of the leopard *(Panthera pardus)* of Africa and Asia. The chief theory as to their genesis in Britain goes back to a piece of legislation called The Dangerous Wild Animals Act. Before this became law in 1976 it was possible for anyone, with the money, to keep almost any species of animal, no matter how dangerous, as a pet. The act stipulated that owners must prove they could keep their charges safely and that they pay a hefty license fee. Many owners merely released their pets into the wild where they thrived and bred. In Africa leopards are preyed on by crocodiles and lions. They must compete with hyenas and hunting dogs. The puma must contend with wolves, wolverine, and bears. In Britain there are no such constraints. With a health population of prey such as deer, rabbits and wildfowl Britain provides the ideal habitat.

Zoologist Chris Moiser, formerly of Plymouth CFE has uncovered evidence that the British big cats may have been around far longer than anybody realised. Amazingly right up until 1981 anyone, no matter how incompetent, could start a zoo! In Victorian days travelling menageries with horse drawn cages containing wild animals were com-

mon place. These slapdash affairs would tour the country and many escapes were recorded.

Regardless of their origin it seems that the British big cats are here for keeps. With consistent reports for decades it is obvious they are breeding here. Evidence is amassing constantly. Big cats have been convincingly filmed and photographed (although many proported images show domestic moggies). Livestock has been killed in unmistakably feline fashion. Paw prints have been taken. Most telling, however, is the undeniable fact that exotic cats have been caught and killed in Britain

In 1980 the late Ted Noble captured a female puma on his farm near Cannich, Scotland. She lived comfortably for the rest of her days in the Highland Wildlife Park. No less than five Indian leopard cats *(Prionailurus bengalensis)* (not to be confused with leopards) have been shot up and down the country from the Scottish borders to Dartmoor. These are spotted cats twice the size of a domestic. Two specimens of the lynx like swamp cat *(Felis chaus)* that hails from India to the middle east, were killed by cars under a year apart in Hampshire and Shropshire. In 1927 a farmer trapped a true lynx *(Lynx lynx)* in Inverness-shire, Scotland.

Catflaps! is a truly unique book, the first and only book dealing with mystery cats in the North East of England, an area very dear to my heart. Andy Roberts, whose name will be familiar to any student of the strange, examines each of the major cases in turn with considerable scholarship. Again and again the pattern repeats itself: a huge cat appears, terrifies witnesses than after a few weeks seems to disappear into thin air. Written with both humour and dedication *Catflaps!* is truly a lost Fortean masterpiece and it is an honour for the Centre for Fortean Zoology to reprint it.

It has been 15 years since *Catflaps!* was written. Now no one can seriously deny the existence of these creatures. All across the country the sightings continue. An update of the area covered by *Catflaps!* would require a whole book (and this humble narrator has spent several nights in deepest Yorkshire woodland hunting the Beast of Selby). What is clear is that though flaps come and go the cats are here to stay and the beasts of the north east will always return.

Richard Freeman
The Centre for Fortean Zoology
Exeter
February 2001

The cover from the original 1986 edition of this book.

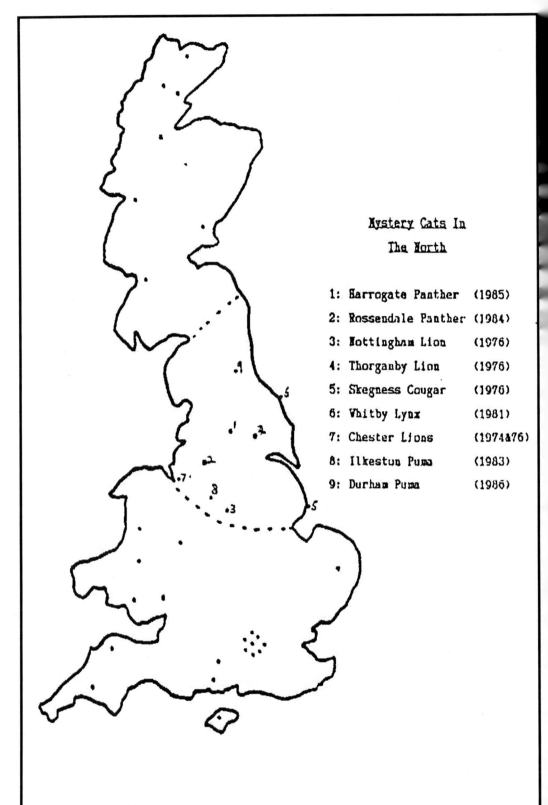

Mystery Cats In The North

1: Harrogate Panther (1985)

2: Rossendale Panther (1984)

3: Nottingham Lion   (1976)

4: Thorganby Lion   (1976)

5: Skegness Cougar   (1976)

6: Whitby Lynx   (1981)

7: Chester Lions   (1974&76)

8: Ilkeston Puma   (1983)

9: Durham Puma   (1986)

● = Other Major Mystery Cat Sighting Locations In The British Isles

INTRODUCTION

Mystery Big Cats have been widely reported from most parts of the British Isles for twenty-five years now, with intermittent sightings having occurred over the course of the past one hundred years. Further back than this, we have a wealth of folk-tales and legends dealing with unusual cats of many types. Latterly, the `Surrey Puma` in the mid-1960s was the first such creature to really capture the media's attention; and in more recent years, the `Beast of Exmoor` and the various Scottish cats have often been in the news.

In the many small-circulation magazines which abound in the Fortean, Paranormal and Earth Mysteries fields, the phantom feline has featured more and more prominently; and two nationally-distributed commercial magazines (*The Unknown* and *Exploring the Supernatural*) regularly feature articles on the subject. *

Theories are rife as to what these creatures actually are and range from the tall tales told by country folk who have had too much to drink, to escaped and released pets and the simple misidentification of wild cats and dogs. The press have often taken up these stories, sometimes treating the subject seriously, sometimes not. Often a mystery cat report will only warrant a few column inches, the story being dropped in a day or two with no satisfactory conclusion having been drawn.

Meanwhile, farmers, policemen and members of the public all over the country are still seeing these animals. Some people take them for granted now; others will not admit to having seen them for fear of ridicule. But the sightings continue. The mystery doesn't stop at sightings either – these cats scratch trees and fences, leave droppings and paw prints, occasionally kill or maim livestock and have even been photographed. Unfortunately, they have avoided capture and no carcasses have been discovered. †

On the other side of the coin lie the more bizarre explanations for the

---

*Sadly, these publications closed down many years ago
†Andy is not quite right in saying no British big cats have been captured. See Richard Freeman's forward for details on Felicity the Scottish puma etc.

11

existence of these mystery felines. Ghost cats, black dog legends, witchcraft and shape-shifting all appear in this booklet in conjunction with these cats. The subject is a folklorist's paradise and sightings of mystery cats are rapidly overtaking that other enigma of the twentieth century – the UFO; and are at least as interesting. Some UFOs apparently even share the same habitat as the mystery cats in the Rossendale case. Recently, Devon naturalist Di Francis's book *Cat Country: The Quest For The British Big Cat*, (1983) has gone a long way towards proving the case for the existence of an indigenous species of hitherto unknown cat (in Scotland and Wales, at least); and in May 1986 a BBC TV *Tomorrow's World* special put forward the theory that exotic big cats were at large in the British countryside (albeit escapees) and that some of the mystery Scottish cats were a hybrid between escaped domestic cats and the indigenous wild cats. No mystery feline has been caught in England as yet though.

In this modest booklet I have attempted to bring together, for the first time, all of the information available about the mystery feline in northern England – an area stretching from north Nottingham- shire to the Scottish Borders. I do not claim this book to be a fully comprehensive collection of mystery cat information (for example, material on the Melrose and North Berwick Puma is absent); but to the best of my knowledge this is the first time that so much material dealing with the Northern Mystery Cat has been gathered together and published.

The information has been gleaned from many places: first-hand reports, newspaper files, on-site investigations and folklore sources, to name but a few. Some of the material has appeared before: in Janet & Colin Bord's excellent book *Alien Animals*, (1980)., for instance, and the British mystery feline saga is regularly chronicled in the indispensable *Fortean Times*. Much of the material is freshly gathered, however, and presented here for the first time, both as an aid to future mystery feline researchers and for those who are just curious about one of England's many modern mysteries. Throughout the book, the terms used to describe the mystery cats such as `Whitby Lynx`, are those used by the media and adopted for convenience. Each case is described initially in terms of eye-witness accounts, official reaction and media reports at the time, with little or no comment as to the nature of the creature seen. This aspect is dealt with in a separate chapter.

NOTE ON NEWSPAPER SOURCES

The 'facts' drawn from newspaper sources are open to many interpretations and the amount of reliance which should be placed on them is open to argument. They are the major source of information from which to compile a book of this type – especially when a case is being looked at which happened a few years ago. Some newspapers carried reports on a particular mystery cat in only one edition; some ran the same basic report in all one day's editions (but with the story changing a little in some cases and in others quite radically). Some of the newspaper accounts included quotes from unnamed witnesses, which does not help when trying to compile an objective account of the mystery cat phenomena. Journalists generally seem to be very unhelpful, or at least unsympathetic, to anyone enquiring into their sources and validity of facts (several letters I sent to various journalists in the course of the research for this book were ignored). Generally, though, the witnesses I spoke to and corresponded with (together with other independently acquired facts), seemed to back up what was reported in the newspapers.

In the course of this research, it was often noted that in a case where a mystery cat was seen many times, the local newspaper only ran one or two pieces on it even though the local inhabitants were all very concerned and the national and regional press were all carrying several items on the case. `The Harrogate Panther` is a case in point here, with only one item appearing in the local paper; whereas the regionals and nationals covered the story extensively. Even the newspaper concerned thought that they had published 'many' articles on the subject when only one actually existed. Press coverage – or the lack of it – may contribute to the amount of sightings in an area, and in some cases create them. This facet of the phenomena is dealt with elsewhere in the book.

CHAPTER ONE

THE HARROGATE PANTHER

EARLY SIGHTING

The story behind the `Harrogate Panther`, which was seen on many occasions in the autumn of 1985, really begins in the small north Yorkshire hamlet of Lower Marshes, near Malton, in early September 1985. The details did not come out until after the `Harrogate Panther` itself was making the news (but it is very likely the first sighting of the creature on record for the area.

At the time of the October/November `Harrogate Panther` sightings, Mrs Jennifer Pool, a farmer's wife, telephoned her local radio station with details of a sighting which had occurred several weeks earlier. Apparently, a group of five young farmers had seen what they described as a *"...Black Panther with orange eyes and a long black tail disappearing into a cornfield close to her home..."* at 11.00 a.m. in the morning. Mrs Pool and her husband inspected the cornfield on the following morning and discovered that a wide path had been made through it at the spot where the young farmers had seen the 'panther'. No tracks were found but the Pool's said that the path was too wide to have been made by either a dog or a fox. [1]

A check with the nearby Flamingo Park Zoo, which keeps a number of big cats, revealed that all of their animals were caged and none had escaped. Mrs Pool had this to say about the young farmers' September sighting: *"The people who saw this are country folk. They know a dog or a fox when they see one. This thing was certainly not a dog or a fox."*

First sightings of the `Harrogate Panther` or not, the above-account follows the 'normal' pattern of events and one which is repeated throughout the `Harrogate Panther` saga. A person or group of people who have experience in animal identification or general observation skills, see an animal which they know is not anything in their normal field of reference. This animal is then described as a panther or a puma or some other big cat; local zoos are checked to no avail, and the police can similarly find no trace of the animal (which then vanishes without trace).

The young farmers' description of what they saw – whilst being vaguely cat-like – does not really describe a Black Panther. There are some similarities with the Black Dog of early British folklore and these will be discussed in a separate chapter.

THE PANTHER COMES TO HARROGATE

The Starbeck and Bilton Hall areas of Harrogate lie off the A59 road between Harrogate itself and Knaresborough.

The land is comprised of farmland and woodland with small fields, tall hedges and is criss-crossed with footpaths, making it a popular area for dog walkers (many of whom were witnesses to the `Harrogate Panther`). At both ends of the area, it is open countryside to both the north and south of Harrogate.

The first sightings of the mystery animal at Harrogate were made in this area of countryside in early October 1985, some three or four weeks after the Low Marishes sighting thirty miles to the north.

Up to twenty people in all reported having seen what they thought was a panther or a puma; but it was only possible to trace three witnesses who were willing to be interviewed. Here follows an account of – and brief comment on – what each witness saw.

MR CLIFFORD'S SIGHTING

The main witness to the `Harrogate Panther` is one Mr Richard Clifford of Starbeck, Harrogate. Mr Clifford is an active eighty-year-old retired farmer who now keeps a smallholding just off the A59 Harrogate-to-Knaresborough road. Mr Clifford saw the mystery animal at least half a dozen times on various occasions during the day in October 1985. All of the sightings were in clear weather conditions and from a distance of about forty yards. Mr Clifford described the animal he saw as being the size of a small Alsatian dog, with a long tail and a low slung belly. The creature was jet black with a short-haired, shiny coat. Mr Clifford, who in his eighty years has had great experience in hunting and general animal identification, said he thought that the animal was a 'puma' and was convinced that it was a 'big cat' of some kind and not a fox, badger or dog.

The mystery animal was seen in the fields adjoining Mr Clifford's smallholding, running across the fields and jumping into and sitting amongst the branches of an old oak tree. Mr Clifford is certain that the animal was 'nesting' in the tree and I was told that a 'den' of some sort was later found there and also that scratches were found on the tree trunk. [2]

When I visited the site and inspected the tree, I could not find any trace of either a 'den' or any scratch marks. If these did originally exist, the previous winter would have dealt harshly with them.

The tree itself was at least thirty feet tall, with the lower branches not starting until twelve or thirteen feet from the floor. It would have been impossible for a domestic dog to have climbed or jumped so high. A

Richard Clifford indicating where he saw the 'Panther'

domestic cat, likewise, could not have made a clean jump into the branches (as was seen); although one could have run up the tree bark. A puma could have done so with ease.

Despite having observed the mystery animal on many occasions for periods of up to several minutes and being certain that it was a big cat of some description, Mr Clifford is still puzzled about some aspects of the animal's behaviour. For instance, Mr Clifford knew that if an animal of this type was living in the vicinity, there would be evidence of its eating habits, such as rabbit carcasses and the like. Although he looked for these signs in the fields in which the animal was seen, none could be found, nor were any prints found which could be attributed to an unknown animal. The creature, whatever it was, disappeared from the locality (and apparently off the face of the Earth) after the intense media interest later in the month of October; and Mr Clifford is of the opinion that one of the many gamekeepers in the area would have shot it and buried the carcass, telling no-one. In fact, Mr Clifford wishes that he had his gun with him on one of the many occasions he saw the creature. Sad though it may be, a carcass would have settled the business once and for all. [3]

Farmer Clifford's account of his sightings must be given careful consideration. Here we have a man who has spent most of his long life engaged in farming and country pursuits and who knows about the identification of all animals indigenous to the area. In spite of this knowledge, he cannot identify a creature he sees half a dozen times or more as anything other than some kind of 'big cat', namely a puma. Perhaps Mr Clifford could have misidentified a feral cat once but not, surely, more than that and at such close range. This dichotomy between observer reliability and actual evidence occurs in all of the witnesses to the `Harrogate Panther`.

BRIAN COOPER'S SIGHTING

Brian Cooper of Forrest Lane Head, Harrogate, is the second witness to the Harrogate Panther. Mr Cooper saw the animal in early October (the same period in which Mr Clifford's sightings occurred and in the same set of fields). Mr Cooper saw the animal once on a clear and sunny afternoon at 3.00 p.m. from a distance of about 250 yards and for a period of about ten minutes.

He described what he saw as a *"...big black cat on the ground...my Jack Russell dog chased it into a tree, barking furiously..."* He thought he had seen a puma: *"A puma, low slung belly and a very long tail."* As for size, Mr Cooper estimated it to be: *"...three times the size of a domestic cat..."*

The tree into which the cat jumped was then chased by Mr Cooper's dog was the same tree in which it was supposed to be living. According to Mr Cooper, the animal jumped *"...a good ten feet up the tree trunk and disappeared among [the] branches"*.

The tree in which the 'Panther' had its lair

Mr Cooper's wife also saw the animal but from too great a distance to be sure of exact details. She is sure, however, that it was a cat of some kind. [3] Mr Cooper's sighting has many identical features to that of Mr Clifford's. The area in which the creature was seen is the same, as is the tree up which the animal climbed when chased. Also, the description is nearly identical, with the creature being black in colour and having a long tail and low slung belly in both accounts. Obviously, both Mr Clifford and Mr Cooper had seen the same animal – and a physical animal is strongly suggested by the fact of Mr Cooper's dog barking at it and chasing it up the tree. Again, Mr Cooper has an occupation in which it is desirable to be able to report facts clearly and rationally. He is a retired police officer. [4]

MR MATTHEWS' SIGHTING

The third witness to the `Harrogate Panther` is Mr C.T. Matthews of Forrest Lane Head, Harrogate. Mr Matthews is an auctioneer, members of which profession are not noted for their lack of quick reactions and observational skills.

At lunchtime on a warm and cloudy Sunday afternoon in October 1985, Mr Matthews saw the mystery animal. Again, the animal was in the same fields as in the previous sightings; and Mr Matthews watched the creature for five minutes from a distance of about one hundred and twenty yards as it entered the field and skirted the perimeter before exiting near to its point of entry. The animal passed close to a diseased rabbit but appeared uninterested in it. Mr Matthews described the animal as being black and the size of a large cat. He thought it was a *"young puma"* (without giving reasons for this assumption) [5].

As in the previous two sightings, an unknown animal (on this occasion described as a puma) was seen in the same fields as the other unknown animal and again by a witness of some credibility.

Besides the above three sightings, the mystery animal was seen by many other people, some of who reported their sighting to the police and some to the media. One of the other people to have seen the creature was the steward of Harrogate Golf Club, Mr Derek Hall, who also found some prints in one of the golf course's bunkers. In an attempt to identify the tracks he contacted Neville Wilby, the curator of Flamingo Park Zoo, who advised Mr Hall of the best way to take plaster casts; but who was unable to accurately identify the prints from a telephone conversation. Mr Wilby was of the opinion, however, that the description of the prints fitted that of an endemic species and suggests a badger. I was unable to contact Mr Hall personally; and as Mr Wilby did not hear from him, I assume that casts were not made. [6]

The media did not pick up on the `Harrogate Panther` story until sightings of the creature had almost ceased (at the end of October and the beginning of November). The local newspaper, *The Harrogate Advertiser* ran a half-page story on the sightings together with photographs of Mr Clifford pointing towards the tree in which the cat was said to be living, and of police searching the undergrowth for signs of the animal. [7]

The regional papers, *The Yorkshire Post* and *The Yorkshire Evening Post* featured at least four news items on the search for the mystery animal and several of the nationals (notably the *Daily Express*, which seems to have a 'thing' about mystery cats) also ran short pieces. The `Harrogate Panther` story was reported objectively and fairly in all the newspapers with hardly an exaggeration or an untruth. Surprisingly, the local paper only had one piece in total on a saga which ran for a couple of weeks elsewhere. Perhaps the panther was reading the news, too, because it disappeared shortly after the bulk of the stories were published.

Besides the media several other bodies were interested in the `Harrogate Panther` too. The police, having received more than a few reports that a panther was on the loose, brought the long arm of the law to bear on the creature. Mounted police, dog handlers and intensive foot patrols scoured the Starbeck and Bilton areas and a vet was put on stand-by with a tranquillising rifle during the search, but nothing could be found to account for the sightings. I was also told that a police helicopter was used in the search but I have been unable to verify this. [8]

The police obviously took the possibility of there being a real big cat in the vicinity very seriously. Besides undertaking a search on such a large scale, it was the police who informed the Press of the animals' presence in order to let the public and farming community know. Had there been any doubt as to the reality of a creature existing in the area, such information would doubtless not have been released (nor would such a large-scale search have been undertaken). In a letter to me, T. Solan, the Chief Inspector of the North Yorkshire Police Force, acknowledged that they had many sightings of an unidentified animal; but were *"…unable to confirm the type of animal involved, as to whether it was a domestic, a native wild animal, or indeed an exotic animal such as a panther"*. [9]

The regional R.S.P.C.A. at Leeds were informed (presumably by the police) of the likelihood of the presence of a panther; although they did not become directly involved with the search [10] Even Harrogate's Principle Environmental Officer, Mr David Hornsey, visited the scene of the search; but the mystery animal had no respect for a big title and refused to appear.

Not far away from the area of the big cat sightings is Knaresborough Zoo; a small-scale affair run by Mr Nick Nyoka *, who is one of Great Britain's acknowledged experts on Big Cats of all varieties. Mr Nyoka's Big Cats had been checked at the time of the Low Marishes sighting and later during the Harrogate sightings; but as is usually the case, none were missing. However, at the time of the Harrogate Panther sightings, Mr Nyoka's zoo was under threat of closure by the local council, who said that the zoo did not meet with various standards (which had recently been introduced and which contributed to the closure of many small zoos like the one at Knaresborough. Mr Nyoka took a very personal view of the Harrogate Panther and thought that the whole thing was a rumour put around to try and discredit his zoo [11] Whether or not this is true is open to question; but one lady I spoke to did tell me: *"They all come from Knaresborough Zoo, you know."* [12] Of course, it was all a rumour and the R.S.P.C.A., notably Sid Jenkins, now made famous by a BBC TV documentary series, saw to it that all of Mr Myoka's big cats were dealt with correctly. Rumour, yes, but the zoo could have contributed to the type of witness climate where it became 'easy' to see a panther or whatever. More of this later.

Ron Deaton, Vertebrate Zoology Group Leader of the Harogate & District Naturalists Society, who has spent over twenty years studying the wildlife in the Harrogate area, was certain that the creature was a mis-perceived feral cat or possibly a mink. He backed this up by noting the lack of droppings, prints, signs of kills etc. Mr Deaton went on to say that over the years he has had all kinds of animals reported to him as being indigenous to the Nidd Gorge – a beauty spot adjoining land where the Harrogate Panther was seen. Mr Deaton's conclusion was that members of the public, whilst being well-meaning are not very adept at animal identification and are apt to exaggerate that which can be otherwise easily identified by a trained observer. [13]

---

* Saldy, Mr Nyoka is now dead, amd the Knaresborough Zoo closed in 1985

CHAPTER TWO

THE ROSSENDALE LION

The `Rossendale Lion` affair is probably the most important of the mystery cat sightings to have occurred in the north of England. It is the only case in the north in which livestock was allegedly killed or maimed by the anomalous creature; and the subsequent saga of the Rossendale beast (that also involves a witch and UFOs) takes us further from the possibility of a 'real' cat and into the realms of folklore. Although the latter two developments really should be covered in the chapter on folklore, they are integral to this story and will be dealt with here.

Rossendale is a collection of valleys on the fringes of the Pennines hill-chain about fourteen miles north-east of Manchester. The valley bottoms are heavily populated; but in a matter of minutes, you can be on the high moor-land which surrounds the area. It was on farmland bordering this moor-land where the `Rossendale Lion` had its brief moment of glory.

As with the Harrogate Panther sightings, the first sighting of the `Rossendale Lion` only came to light in retrospect. Fourteen-year-old Bury schoolboy Owen Jepson was the first – and one of the very few-people to see the beast. Two months before the August 1984 sightings he had seen a mysterious creature and was quoted as saying: *"I just saw its back legs and tail as it jumped over some rushes. The tracks were cat prints. I got books out of the library and decided that it only matched up with a mountain lion."* No-one took Owen's sighting seriously at first; and it was forgotten about until some sheep killings were attributed to a mountain lion. [1])

The killings occurred on a fifty-acre holding (Hawthorn Farm) belonging to farmer, Geoff Dootson, and situated at Whitewell Bottom. The sheep had had the flesh completely stripped from the carcasses and a cow was mauled. Mr Dootson also caught sight of the creature and described it thus: *"It is sable-coloured, similar to a lion."*

With the possibility of animal killings, the police became involved; and searches (fruitless as usual) were made of the Whitewell Bottom and the Scoutbottom Moor areas, both on foot and by mounted police, and aided by local farmers armed with sticks. The acting police chief of Rossendale, David Nutter, advised people to keep off the moors saying: *"We have had reports that would suggest there is a possibility that it is some kind of large cat. If it is we have no idea where is can have come from. Until we establish what it is, I would advise people to stay away from the area. At this moment we do not know what it is."* Elsewhere, an unnamed police spokesman was more definite as to the existence of the creature: *"People are advised to keep away from the area while this wild animal is at large."*

Tracks, purportedly from the mystery creature, were found on St Naze Hill and the mammal curator of Chester Zoo, Peter Wait, was called in to inspect them. After seeing the prints, which were somewhat dried out in a patch of mud, Mr Wait pronounced his verdict: *"Definitely dog prints. These were not made by a big cat."* The prints may have only been of a dog, but Mr wait did not rule out an animal of more exotic origins: *"If there is a puma up here I'm afraid they'll have to shoot him. After a while living wild they become very cunning and almost impossible to trap alive. Nowadays all dangerous cats must be li-*

censed and none has been reported missing." If there was a puma or something like it living on the moors, Mr Wait's comments were correct because despite all-night vigils by armed farmers and the setting of traps baited with dead sheep, nothing was caught and nothing more was seen of the `Rossendale Lion`. [2]

SHAPE SHIFTING.

One of the more bizarre explanations for the existence of the Rossendale creature was given by Manchester woman Mrs Barbara Brandolini. Mrs Brandolini was, and no doubt still is, a witch, who at the time headed a coven in Manchester. At the time of the `Rossendale Lion` saga, Mrs Brandolini (whose witch name is *Margansa*) and her coven were attempting to buy an old Baptist chapel at Slack, next to Hepstonall, high on the moors above Hebden Bridge in West Yorkshire and only ten miles or so away from the scene of the Rossendale events. Margansa and her friends wanted to buy the old chapel with a view to turning it into an occult temple and were at the time receiving stiff opposition from local vicars and the like who had visions of hordes of naked pagans getting loose in the ex-house of God! Seizing a chance for a bit of free publicity, Margansa, in a radio interview on the fifteenth of August, claimed that she was responsible for the sheep killings in Rossendale. How was she responsible? Was she the owner of an errant mountain lion, perhaps? Nothing so simple...Margansa claimed that she had actually become the panther and done the dirty deed. Threatening to do the same again, she said: *"I will appear as a big cat in Hepstonstall. People tend to think it all belongs in books and so on but it does not. It is very real."* [3]

The following evening's *Halifax Evening Courier* reported that no panthers, black or otherwise, had been seen in Hepstonstall on the previous night; although, strange animal noises had been heard. Incidentally, Mrs Brandolini's publicity stunt backfired on her; and due to the hue and cry she created, the Chapel was sold to God-fearing Christians instead. Mrs Brandolini faded from prominence; although she was still claiming that she had shape-shifted into the Rossendale animal in August of this year. [4]

UNIDENTIFIED FLYING OBJECTS

The local people of Rossendale held many opinions as to what the mystery creature actually was. Some thought it was just a dog, most likely a Great Dane; whilst others held more exotic theories. Amongst them was the widespread local belief that wild lynxes were responsible for the killings and had been roaming the moors above the Rossendale Valley for the past five years, living in caves in one of the quarries on the edge of the Moor. [5]

The quarries are all located above the Rossendale village of Stacksteads, about five miles from the Whitwell Bottom area. This connection with the creatures allegedly living in quarries is intriguing; if only from the point of view of a rumour, as in the late 1970s, Rossendale was host to another visitation from unexplained phenomena, this time in the shape of a UFO flap. This has been well-covered in many places, notably Jenny Randles's book *The Pennine UFO Mystery*, and various UFO magazines. Briefly, hundreds of UFOs were seen in the Rossendale area with more than a few being seen flying over - and appearing to land in – the very quarries where the locals thought the mystery lynx could be living. Rossendale tailor, Mike Sacks, saw such a UFO apparently land in one of the quarries and drove up to take a better look – and upon doing so, saw something in the quarry which he thought could not have been of earthly manufacture. The UFO flap lasted considerably longer than the mystery animal flap, and needless to say, no UFO was ever actually found to have accounted for the wealth of sightings. [6]

Although animals were allegedly killed by the Rossendale creature, local farmers were very alarmed and the police and various 'experts' were brought in, the killings only merited one mention in a local newspaper, *The Rossendale Free Press*. Most of the nationals picked up on the story, calling the animal variously a lion, mountain lion, cougar, panther, puma and lynx, not to mention the 'pet' names given to it – such as the *Daily Express's* `Beast of Bacup`, for which article the journalist who covered the case for the Express couldn't resist changing his by-line to William (Great White) Hunter! By the end of August, the `Beast of Bacup` had vanished whence it came.

CHAPTER THREE

THE NOTTINGHAMSHIRE LION

The north was a hotbed of mystery cat activity long before the Harrogate and Rossendale flaps, and to find the first and biggest of these flaps we must go back to 1976 and the county of Nottinghamshire.

The spate of sightings is recorded, wrongly as it turns out, as beginning at Tollerton, a Nottingham suburb, opposite Nottingham Airport, when two milkmen reported seeing a lion. Mr David Crowther had just delivered milk to a bungalow when he saw the animal. His fellow worker, Mr David Bentley, said: *"Dave stopped half-way down the drive and was obviously looking at something. I shouted to him to ask what was the matter and he told me to come and look. He said there was something prowling about; and then we both saw together what certainly to us was a lion. It was fifty yards away, had its head down and its long tail had a bushy end. It was walking away from us but only very slowly."*

The two milkmen attempted to get other witnesses to the lion's presence by awakening nearby residents; but by the time that they returned, the animal, whatever it was, had gone. After reporting the sighting to the police – who were at first sceptical – Chief Inspector John Smith ordered a full-scale search to be carried out. A police helicopter was brought in along with marksmen; and police with loud-hailers toured the area warning the public. Locals in the area reported that their dogs had been *"mysteriously restless"* during the previous night and a farmer at Clipstone said he had seen strange paw prints on his land. [1]

Following the publicity given to the above-sightings, other members of the public came forward and reported several sightings of a mysterious cat-like animal; all of which took place before the date of the Tollerton sighting. Police received eighteen calls and included amongst them were a sighting from a couple who saw a lion in a lay-by but didn't report it for fear of not being believed; and a sighting from a farmworker at Edwalton, who saw a lion in a field. Local vet Miss Mary

Guilor calmly suggested that anyone encountering the lion should not panic and advised people to keep their pets – especially dogs – indoors. [2]

By the third day of the hunt, many more sightings had been phoned in to the police; the lion (or lions!) now having been seen in two places at the same time – even on the M1 slip-road at Ratclife-on-Soar. The Chief Constable of Nottinghamshire, Mr Charles McLachan, said he was *"amazed"* at the response from the public who were apparently telephoning from as far away as Liverpool offering help and advice – including a man who owned twenty lions and who wanted to use one as a lure; suggestions that Jack Russell terriers (!) should be used in the hunt; and someone else suggesting the possibility of leaving food out for the creature in case it was hungry. As no livestock had been reported killed, the creature was probably hungry; but even Ladbrokes the bookmakers, who were getting in on the act by offering odds of 3-1 against a lion being captured by midnight on the following Saturday, weren't going to make much of a killing. Perhaps they knew something no-one else did. [3] [4]

On August 1st, the animals' tenuous reality status was given a boost when the deputy coroner for Nottinghamshire, Dr John Chisholm, "convinced" police that there was a big animal at large. Dr Chisholm and his wife were walking on land near their home at Normanton-on-the-Wolds when Dr Chisholm heard a noise near a stream. Upon investigating the source of the noise, he saw the rear end of an animal resembling a lion trying to force its way through some undergrowth. Dr Chisholm's wife thought it was trying to get to the stream. They went back to their house and from an upstairs window saw the animal leaving the area. Dr Chisholm's sighting rekindled the search and again police toured the area warning residents to keep windows and doors closed and children inside. Armed police officers were stationed at strategic points in the area, with patrols being increased at dusk – the police working on the theory that the animal would lie low during the daytime, daring only to emerge after darkness had fallen. [5]

Reports were also received from other areas, notably Nicker Hill, Keyworth, where two women had allegedly seen *"something"* in a field. *"Something"* turned out to be nothing but led the police to express alarm at the lack of care being taken by the public; fifty of whom, including many children, were searching for the mystery creature when the police arrived on the scene. [6] As the saga moved into its second week, the number of sightings recorded by the police approached sixty, with sightings still coming in. More sightings of a lion were reported from the Tollerton area and police patrols continued. Nottingham Racecourse was searched after a man reported seeing a *"sandy-coloured animal like a young lioness"* in a field near the racecourse – but police found nothing. [7]

On the 6th of August, the police announced that they no longer thought a lion was on the loose, but would continue to respond to sightings of the now non-existent creature. The police now went back on all their previous certainty that a lion was in the area and began to explain some of the sightings as large dogs and suchlike; one witness was even said to have confused a paper bag with a lion! An unnamed 'expert' from an equally-unnamed local safari park reassured the public, saying that no evidence whatsoever had been found to suggests that a real, bona-fide lion had ever been loose in the area; and the police continued to back this new theory up, saying that police had no reports of any lions escaping from captivity. Lion fever gradually subsided and Ladbrokes stopped taking bets. [8]

On the 7th August, the *Nottingham Evening Press* carried its last news item on the lion. The scare was over. *The Nottingham Lion* scare was the first multi-witness sighting of a modern day mystery cat in the north and it certainly wouldn't be the last. A further, isolated, mystery cat sighting took place at Ilkeston (only a few miles from Nottingham) in 1983; and further east a 'cougar' was seen at Skegness. Perhaps the Nottinghamshire Lion took up travelling - after all it was seen on the M1 slip-road! [8]

CHAPTER FOUR

THE THORGANBY LIONESS

As the Nottinghamshire Lion saga drew to a close, media attention shifted to the Yorkshire village of Thorganby, nine miles south of York. *"Lioness at large hunt draws blank,"* proclaimed the *Yorkshire Evening Post* of 10th August (the first paper to report the story) and it went onto detail the sighting.

The witness, Mr Alan Pestell (Pestill or Pestall in some accounts), was walking down the village main street on the 9th August, towards the local pub. It was dark, but the road was well lit by bright moonlight in which Mr Pestell saw what he later described to the police as a "lioness" which disappeared into a field of stubble at the side of the main street. [1]

In the following night's newspapers, a full account of Mr Pestell's sighting appeared and he was quoted as saying: *"I left home at 9.55 p.m. The evening was dark, but the centre of the road was well lit by the moon. Out of the shadows came what I first thought was a dog, but as I got close I froze. It stared at me as it padded past, and I stepped into the light to look at it. I was amazed – it was a large lioness!"* Mr Pestell spoke to the creature, but on realising that he was confronting a lioness, walked on, fearing to break into a run in case whatever it was jumped on his back.

After seeing the creature, Mr Pestell continued his journey to the pub where his story apparently met with disbelief. This didn't seem to bother him, though, and he said: *"Look, I saw a lioness and that's all that bothers me. I've got three young kids and a wife to worry about, and I'm not about to make things up."* [2]

Police searched the area on the following day using tracker-dogs; and house-to-house enquiries were made at farms and cottages; but no lioness was found, nor were there any large dogs reported missing which could have accounted for the sighting. A police spokesman said:

"This was an isolated reported sighting of a lioness walking into a field. A search was made by police with dog but there have been no other sightings. All local zoos, including Flamingo Park and Knaresborough have been checked and no animals are missing."

As the police said, no more sightings of the `Thorganby Lioness` were reported. The incident made several news reports in the *Yorkshire Evening Post*. The sightings were soberly reported even though there was a direct mention of a pub in the account. As an adjunct, it is perhaps worth noting that a year earlier, in 1975, a milkman saw an animal he described as a bear on Skipwith Common just a few miles away from Thorganby. This, too, was a one-off sighting which was never explained. [3]

CHAPTER FIVE

THE SKEGNESS COUGAR.

Nineteen-seventy-six was a bumper year for mystery cat sightings in the north; and less than two months after the Nottingham Lion scare, police were again busy investigating reports of an out-of-place big cat. This time a cougar had been seen in the Lincolnshire seaside resort of Skegness.

The alleged cougar was seen roaming the grounds of Seely House (a Skegness sea-front convalescent home) late in the afternoon of the 20th of September, by Dr Alec Jamieson, the Skegness police surgeon. Dr Jamieson was quoted in the local papers as saying: *"It was a large cat about five feet long and sandy coloured; definitely a cougar."*

The police were called in and the creature was also seen by Police Constable Jock Gartshore, his description echoing that of Dr Jamieson's, in that he said it was *"...a large cat about the size of a Labrador..."* Police searching the grounds of the convalescent home came up with evidence of something in the shape of several large paw prints measuring two-and-a-half inches by three inches; unfortunately, the local newspaper does not report whether these prints were of a cougar or something more mundane. [1]

Some of the staff at Seely House reported having seen the animal on many occasions over the preceding weeks and they thought it was a large dog. Baffled, the police brought in an R.S.P.C.A. inspector, and he, together with local naturalist Mr John Yeadon, hid themselves in the house grounds in the hope of seeing and photographing the elusive beast. We must presume they were unsuccessful as nothing further was reported in the newspapers.

A senior police officer at the time said: *"We are keeping an open mind. Obviously we must take precautions, but from all we have heard it seems that whatever it is, it is not dangerous."* Police surgeon Jamieson ended the *Scunthorpe Evening Telegraph's* report by saying: *"It could well be this cougar which was reported in the Nottinghamshire area."*

The Skegness sightings had, true to form, followed the classic mystery cat pattern. Several people, some of them 'reliable' witnesses such as policemen, saw the creature. Unsubstantiated evidence in the shape of the paw prints was found, but a search proved fruitless. The local press only ran one article on the `Skegness Cougar` and couldn't resist suggesting that the `Nottinghamshire Lion` had taken a *"holiday trip"* to Skegness.

If it had, then Skegness wasn't as bracing as its publicity would have it, for no more was heard of the Skegness Cougar. Perhaps it went back down the coast to the Cromer area, in the county of Norfolk, where mystery cats were seen in 1964 and again in 1975.

Lincolnshire is no stranger to mystery quadrupeds, having probably more Black Dog legends than any other county in Great Britain. These Black Dogs will be discussed in relation to mystery cats in a separate section.

CHAPTER SIX

THE DURHAM PUMA

This is the latest northern cat sighting and occurred as this book was being compiled. Initial reports appear to indicate that it is one of the biggest cat flaps since the 1976 'wave' of mystery cat sightings and has made headline news on Tyne Tees TV on quite a few occasions since the first sighting in early August. Nineteen-eighty-six may prove to be the best year for phantom felines for a long time. Besides the `Durham Cat` (and unfortunately outside the scope of this book), unidentified cats have been sighted numerous times in Scotland, at Thirsk [1] in Yorkshire and further south in the Forest of Dean. `The Beast of Exmoor` has been up to its old tricks again; and Devon naturalist Nigel Brierley has allegedly identified the animal as a brown lynx by paw casts and hairs found on sheep it had killed. `The Durham Cat` deserves – and will probably get – a more detailed on-the-spot investigation from some intrepid Fortean, but until then, I present the details gleaned from newspapers and letters so far.

The first sighting of a mystery animal in the Durham area occurred at the beginning of August when a young couple saw a large cat with a face like a cheetah near their home at Bowburn. [2] No more reports were received until the middle of September, when a motorist driving on the A167 road at the Thinford roundabout, to the south of Durham, saw a large, black unidentified cat, said to be larger than a police dog, run into a field at the rear of the *Thinford Bridge Inn* public house. The animal was seen with a smaller cat. Mystery cats have been seen elsewhere with smaller cats, presumably their offspring. Wales and Surrey are two such places where they have been observed. [3]

Another report which centres on Thinford – and which may or may not be a version of the above account – tells a more fearsome tale. The driver in this account was a lorry driver and the mystery cat jumped onto the windscreen of his cab and snarled at the driver through the window. The driver called for help on his CB radio; but before help could arrive, the cat jumped off and fled when caught in the head-

lights of a car. An ex-Windsor Safari Park warden who lived in the area dismissed claims that the creature was a puma or a black panther and said it was far more likely to have been a large dog or a wild cat.

Just over a week later, the mystery feline hit the headlines again. This time, it was seen by a man walking his Doberman dog in a field near Ferryhill. The witness, Brian Rothery, said that the cat was stalking a group of children who were playing in some sheds: *"There were about nine kids, their ages ranging between seven and ten, playing in some sheds. I saw this black thing and at first I thought it was a small horse, then I realised it was too long to be a horse. It was standing with its head down towards the grass. It could have been stalking the kids judging by the way it was standing."* The children then caught sight of the cat and ran off, shouting. Mr Rothery rushed off to telephone the police but by the time they arrived nothing could be found. Having received reports of a mystery cat from other areas including Fishburn Coke Works and the Dean & Chapter Industrial Estate, Ferryhill, Durham County Police said it was vital that the animal should be located, and the obligatory police spokesman added: *"Everyone appears to be positive about the type of animal it is."* [4]

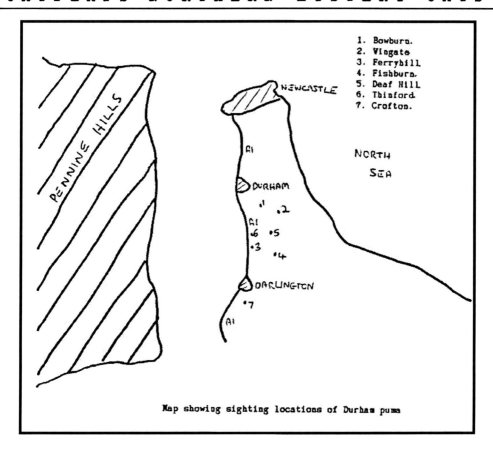

1. Bowburn.
2. Wingate
3. Ferryhill
4. Fishburn.
5. Deaf Hill
6. Thinford
7. Crofton.

Map showing sighting locations of Durham puma

Eddie Bell, a local policeman and naturalist, announced that he, along with the zoologist Dr Nigel Dunston, was going to track the puma to its lair. It had a lair because the R.S.P.C.A. said so and they were watching it through infra-red binoculars! [5]

Despite the long arm of the law on its tail, sightings of the mystery animal continued unabated. Senior citizen Florence Watson of Deaf Hill (Co. Durham) saw the beast whilst hanging out her washing. Before heading off to a nearby quarry, Florence was able to study the creature and described it thus: *"It was quite a bit bigger than an Alsatian, with a cat-like appearance, and was dark brown with a straight neck and pointed ears."* Stop laughing those of you who think it sounds like a Doberman! [6]

Wingate, Co. Durham, was the next port of call for the elusive puma. Arthur Hardy, another 'wildlife enthusiast' and Steven Dodsworth saw the creature, apparently asleep, behind Vingate Auction Sales-room. Arthur Hardy said of the creature: *"It was bigger than an Alsa-tian, jet-black in colour with pointed ears on the top of its head and a very long tail."* Alsatians featured in another Wingate sighting when a large black cat was seen coming out of bushes near a stream, by a man walking his own Alsatian, which wouldn't go near the animal (which was described as being bigger than a dog).

North Yorkshire Police received a sighting report (from the same day that the cat was seen in Wingate), from Croft-on-Tees some fifteen miles south of Wingate, where a 'black panther' had been spotted at 8.00 p.m. by a woman motorist driving on the Middleton Tyas to Croft road. The police, on-the-ball as ever, said the animal could be moving south! [6]

Police Constable Eddie Bell, who had taken ten days holiday to con-tinue his search for the puma at the end of October, presumably with no luck, featured in the newspapers again when he investigated a sighting at Gypsy Lane, between Bradbury Hill and Ferryhill Station. A large black animal, about the size of a Labrador with a long curly tail, had been seen and, according to the *Hartlepool Mail*, was mis-taken by PC Bell for the mystery animal. The animal turned out to be a stray dog and bit PC Bell on the hand before running off!! Undaunted, PC Bell continued his search for the mystery cat, following up a report of a Shildon man who had seen a 'puma' from a train in April. [7]

Superintendent Barry Purdy of the Durham sub-division made an ap-peal to walkers and poachers to report anything which might have led police to the creature's lair. `The Durham Puma`, whatever it was, may have been prepared to give itself up, as a large cat-like creature was seen running behind the police station at Newton Hall. The flap slowed down and by December appeared to have subsided altogether. No doubt many more sightings await discovery in this flap and hope-fully these (and official comments from police, R.S.P.C.A. etc will come to light at a later date). A 'real' cat of some kind may have been the cause of the Durham flap.

The area to the north, south and east of Durham has had cat sightings in the past (Melrose, Berwick, Harrogate, Thirsk and Whitby), and so proponents of any of the 'physical cat' theories may read something into this. The area covered by cat sightings is also consistent with that of the area covered by a hunting cat of some sort.

It is also, however, about the same area covered by a journalistically-stimulated flap, such as those which occurred in the mid-war years involving 'jumping ghosts' and the like. Until we are presented with either a live specimen or a carcass, the `Durham Puma`, like all of the other cats in this book, will remain a mystery.

CHAPTER SEVEN

A CAT MISCELLANY

Besides the preceding mystery cat sightings, there have been a number of other single sightings or less well witnessed sightings of mystery cats in the north of England.

Here follows brief details of those I have managed to locate to date. Others have no doubt occurred and have either been missed or have gone unreported.

Two mystery cat sightings which are not mentioned here due to space restrictions are the sightings at North Berwick and Melrose, in the Scottish Border regions in 1976 and 1983 respectively. In 1986, there were also rumours of a cat-like animal stalking fields near Skipton and Thirsk – both in North Yorkshire. [1]

• THE WHITBY LYNX

In the autumn of 1981, a housewife in Whitby, North Yorkshire, was awakened in the early hours by *"unearthly noises"* and also by the sound of what she later discovered was her garden gate being torn to pieces. At the time, Mrs Rigden thought it was a burglar; but upon inspecting the gate in the morning, she found that it seemed to have been destroyed by an animal. Blood stains and animal hairs were found on the remains of the gate, together with *"fang"* marks in the wood itself.

Mrs Rigden speculated that the creature had become trapped in her small backyard and had had to destroy the gate to get free.

The police were called in but could not offer any explanation and neither could they identify the type of animal which could chew through a gate in such a fashion. The following night, in the same area, a man walking his dog saw two cats fighting with *"unusual ferocity"*; he threw a rock at them and one fled. The other turned to face him and was much bigger than an ordinary cat, with very long legs and pointed ears. It bared large dog-like fangs at him and then slunk off.

The local R.S.P.C.A. was of the opinion that the creature was a lynx and advised people to be careful if they cornered it. The police checked the local zoos without any luck and went on to advise farmers to *"get out the 12-bore and shoot it"*. Apparently, no samples of either the blood or fur were ever analysed and no more was heard from the `Whitby Lynx`. [2]

• THE ILKESTON PUMA

In February 1983, after reading a review of Di Francis's book, Vincent Mizuro of Ilkeston, Derbyshire, wrote to his local newspaper to report his mystery animal sighting.

He had been feeding his two ducks when he noticed something resembling either a large bundle of black fur, or a group of several cats, on a mound about one hundred yards away from him.

He whistled to see if it was alive and the creature stood up, appearing to be about three feet in length with long fur. He described it as being a puma and said that it was much bigger than the stuffed Scottish wild-cats that he had seen. [3]

This was the only report of this particular animal and is very sparse in terms of detail. It is perhaps worth noting that the Ilkeston area is within thirty miles of the area of the 1976 Nottingham Lion sightings.

• THE CHESTER CATS

In May 1974, a mystery animal was often seen in the Delaware Forest area, to the north of Chester. It was described as being around two feet in height, like an Alsatian dog but with a tail like a fox's brush. The witnesses were sure that it was not a fox though.

In the national mystery cat 'wave' of 1976, a lioness was seen in Deva Lane, Chester, very near Chester Zoo. Needless to say, all of Chester Zoo's big cats were accounted for. The creature was seen twice again near the West Chester Hospital. Police searched the area but could find nothing. [4]

Author and journalist Paul Screeton, who supplied me with the Durham cat clippings had his own mystery cat sighting; and is one that suggests another explanation for the origins of the phantom feline phenomenon. The sighting took place on May 8th 1983 when Paul and his friend John Watson were driving through Northumberland.

As they drove through Hulne Park, Alnwick, 'something' crossed the road in front of them. Paul recorded his sighting in the journal of the Northern Earth Mysteries: *"My impression was that a large all-black cat or panther form crossed the road one hundred or so yards ahead of us from left to right and disappeared into the undergrowth. To me it was as tall as an adult Doberman Pinscher, twice the length and lower slung, moving with a powerful, quick feline gait."*

John Watson also saw it but later thought that it was greyish and moved slower. Although these two people, both well-versed in the study of anomalies, saw this out-of-place cat, it did not occur to the driver to stop the car or brake for a better look, nor did Paul think to attempt to use his loaded camera which he had in his pocket.

EDITOR`S NOTE: The lack of action with the camera seen in this case is not so unusual, nor is it indicative of a "paranormal" creature. Jon Downes of the Centre for Fortean Zoology saw the Beast of Bodmin lope across the road in front of his car in broad daylight. He had a camera around his neck but was too amazed to use it!

This 'strangeness' also manifested itself in the fact that Paul didn't really register what the cat did after it crossed the road, only its presence on the road. Also, despite the obvious cat-like appearance of the animal, Paul said: *"Was that a deer?"* after it had vanished from view. This distortion of perception and lack of co-ordination is a feature of other types of anomaly experience – especially in UFO encounters, where it is known as the *Oz Factor*, and it raises even more problems with regard to the 'reality' of what it is seen. To this day, Paul Screeton is not sure exactly what he saw crossing the road – only that he saw something unusual. [5]

• OTHER MYSTERY ANIMALS.

Besides sightings of out-of-place cats, the north of England has been home to mystery animals of many varieties. Kangaroos, Sea-serpents, Bigfoot and Bison are just a few of the other out-of-place creatures seen in the north. However, none of these have appeared with anything like the same regularity as the cats and this does tend to detract from their 'realness'. The sheer volume of cat sightings and the likelihood of many others going unreported continues to add to the weight of evidence for some 'reality'.

CHAPTER EIGHT

MYSTERY CATS IN LEGEND & LORE

A brief look at folktales from the north of England which cover animals that may be related to the mystery cats seen today. The amount of actual truth in the first two is debatable; but together they and a short look at modern folktales throw a little light on how mystery cats have been dealt with and categorised in the popular imagination up to the present day.

• THE FLIXTON "WEREWOLF"

The earliest reference to any kind of vaguely cat-like mystery animal in the north of England occurs in AD 940, when the area around Flixton, East Yorkshire, was visited by a creature that, in the context of this book, would appear to have been a cross between a black dog, a phantom feline and a werewolf.

It was popularly described as possessing abnormally large eyes that glowed in the dark, a long tail and it exuded a terrible stench. The creature also attacked and mutilated livestock, dogs and even people. At the time, tradition had it that the beast was being manipulated by a magician. What this creature was, has never been explained; and as it is so far in the past, it will probably remain so. It seems to contain a good mix of the best parts of both black dog and mystery cat lore. [1]

• THE BARNBOROUGH CAT

St Peter's Church in the small South Yorkshire village of Barnborough has a cat legend attached to it that may well pertain to one of our mystery felines; but if not, then it is certainly testimony to the respect with which England's indigenous cats were held. These we will return to in the final chapter. Briefly, the legend is of a local man, one Percival

Cresacre, who died at the claws of a 'wood cat' in 1475. Riding out from Barnborough through the South Yorkshire countryside in the depths of winter, Percival was accosted by the 'wood cat', which jumped behind him onto his horse's saddle. The horse broke into a gallop and unseated Percy, who then realised the cause of the horse's sudden actions.

The cat flew at him, fastened itself at the back of his shoulders and wounded him terribly. The fight between the two raged as Percival tried to return to Barnborough; several times he almost overcame the cat but was weakened tremendously in the struggle. Upon reaching the church porch, the cat still clinging to him, both of them were totally exhausted; and in a last attempt to kill the creature, Cresacre fell across the cat and crushed the life from it. This final act was to be Percival's last, too, and he died shortly after being discovered by the church acolyte the following morning.

The story of this battle went down in Cresacre family history and is embodied in their crest – still to be seen on the tower of the Church at Barnborough.

A carving of the event can also be seen at the church; and stains on the porch floor are said to be blood stains from the battle. Other writers have interpreted the tale as originating with the Cresacre family to account for their particular coat of arms; and it has also been interpreted in a geomantic sense in terms of Percy Cresacre's journey through the landscape and the places (not mentioned here) he rode through. [2] [3]

- ## THE GIRT DOG OF ENNERDALE

This is another legend that has been interpreted by some anomaly chroniclers as being representative of a mystery cat. In the springtime of 1810, farmers all across the Cumberland area of Ennerdale Water were finding sheep from their flocks slaughtered. A fox was ruled out due to the ferocity and number of the killings and the farmers were on the lookout for a killer dog. The animal responsible for the killings ranged far and wide, never attacking the same flock twice in succession; with no-one being able to predict where it would strike next. The first person to see the creature – a shepherd – said that it was unlike any beast that he had ever seen before: a large, yellow lion-like creature with dark grey stripes. It was thought to be variously a lion; a cross between a mastiff and a greyhound; and even something of su-pernatural origin.

Whatever the creature was, no farmer's dog would approach it; and a pack of hounds, formed especially for the purpose of hunting it down, were also frightened off after the beast had killed several of the lead hounds. The 'Girt Dog' – as it became known – seemed invincible, ig-noring poisoned carcasses and evading the many shepherds armed with guns who scoured the fell-sides in search of it. The 'Girt Dog' was at large throughout the spring and summer of 1810, frequently seen and even more frequently hunted by some of Lakeland's finest hunts-men, but never caught. At least one of the many people who saw the animal was sure that it was a cat of some kind. Will Rotherby was gathering firewood near a field in which the animal had been cornered and being somewhat deaf Rotherby did not hear the ensuing commo-tion. The animal ran towards him, knocking him over and leaving him shaken and with the firm conviction that he had been knocked over not by a dog but by a lion.

The tales of the pursuit of this creature became legendary in hunting circles and no doubt more than a few can be attributed to exaggera-tion. A number of the tales cited above may be the product of the over-active 19th Century journalists' minds and the desire for a sensational story; but there is not doubt that something was killing sheep and evading capture and that something was cat-like. The area over which the killings occurred have led some researchers to believe that more than one animal was at work; but there is no real evidence of this.

On the 12th of September 1810, the sport came to an end and the 'Girt Dog' was at last run to ground and shot. It eventually dragged itself to the Eden river, fending off hounds as it went, and then made a break for some nearby woodland where it was again cornered and shot, the hounds finishing it off. In Fort's book, it is said that it was a dog that was eventually killed and the sheep killings did stop with its death. The carcass of whatever it was – dog or otherwise – was allegedly stuffed and put on display at a Keswick museum, but is now lost. Sheep slaughter by unknown animals also took place in Edale, Derby-shire, in 1925 where something *"...black in colour and of enormous size..."* was roaming around at night. Hunters were unable to find the culprit and the killings stopped as suddenly as they had started. [4] [5]

EDITOR'S NOTE: See the appendix on the `Girt Dog` by Richard Freeman for a theory on the nature of this particular beast.

• BLACK DOGS

The many Black Dog legends that are spread all over the British Isles have given rise to much speculation as to whether or not the Black Dog is one and the same creature as the mystery cat. Various writers have suggested that the two may be the same - Di Francis and the Bord's amongst them; and it would be very convenient for those who believe that the mystery cat has always been with us, if the Black Dog and mystery cats could be linked.

Unfortunately, I don't think that they can. The two types of account bear only superficial resemblance, especially when the accounts from the north of England are studied. Rather than spend pages going through these differences, they are best expressed by the similarities below.

Some similarities can be found – in the movements, for example – which are often described as a 'lope' for both mystery cats and Black Dogs and also in the sizes given by witnesses to both creatures.

The size factor is ambiguous, though, as both have been described as being between two and five feet in height; and one Black Dog account features one that grew to the size of a row of trees (and others have noted Black Dogs that seem to grow and shrink.

COMPARISONS

BLACK DOG.

Colour: *Generally black, with regional variations (white, grey).*

Coat: *'Shaggy'; 'Woolly; 'Sheep-like'.*

Eyes: *'Like huge red saucers'; nearly always noticed.*

Smell: *Often sulphurous. Breath often noted as being unpleasant.*

Sound: *Rarely makes a sound itself but is often heard. Sounds range from 'chain dragging' to 'splashing' sounds. Both common.*

Locations: *Often seen in one place repeatedly over a long period of time. Seen indoors occasionally. Seen at prehistoric sites and similar places. Ley-line connections. Seen mainly on roads, lanes and streets.*

Human Contact: *Witnesses often touched or brushed against the dog. Dog follows or accompanies human often. Dogs seem to seek out humans intentionally.*

'Reality': *Dog frequently seen passing through fences, gates etc. Never caught. Seen as a 'mist' at times. Dogs with two heads, different faces seen.*

Legends: *Pre-sager of death. Guardian and protector. Treasure guardian. Many others.*

MYSTERY CAT

Colour: *Often black. Also striped.*

Coat: *Frequently described as smooth or short-haired.*

Eyes: *Rarely noted but sometimes red and glowing.*

Smell: *Rarely, if ever, noted.*

Sound: *Little, if any, sound noted with mystery cats.*

Locations: *Seen in same places only in 'flaps'. Nearly always seen in countryside. No specific site connections.*

Human Contact: *Little or no contact between mystery cats and people. Cats attempt to avoid human contact.*

'Reality': *Can be chased by dogs. Allegedly kills animals, leaves marks, tracks etc.*

Legends: *No specific legends as yet; although some old cat legends exist; also rise of urban legends, including escaped animals.*

This table only briefly touches on what I think are the disparities between Black Dogs and the Northern Mystery Cat. The individual reader should make up his or her own mind; and the list of references at the back of the book should be consulted for a more accurate account. The Black Dog is a real (and I think) paranormal phenomena. Every town and village within a twenty-mile radius of my home-town (Brighouse) has at least one; and sometimes many Black Dog legends bear no real relation to mystery cat accounts and the situation is repeated all over Yorkshire. Many of the Black Dog tales blend into each other – such as the older legends such as the Hell-Hounds of Scandinavian mythology and the Gabble-Ratchets. Most of them have, I think, similarities with that other well-known paranormal event – the ubiquitous 'Grey Lady' (also a pre-sager of death and a haunter of one specific place over a long period of time – but that is another story altogether). [6] [7] [8]

Suggestions that the mystery cats area paranormal manifestation in the ghost tradition are hard to prove or disprove; but comparing the Black Dog accounts with mystery cat accounts shows up, I think, too many differences. There are exceptions to this, of course, and Paul Screeton's personal 'Black Panther' sighting shows another, rarely reported, side to the mystery cat encounters. This type of cat encounter is so rarely mentioned, however, that it may not be relevant to the other cases in this book; or it could be that genuine 'Ghost Panthers' are part of the mystery cat phenomenon.

• MODERN FOLKLORE.

Modern folklore, or the urban legend. may account for the develop-
ment of some – if not all – of the mystery feline accounts and provides
an easy way of explanation for anyone who doubts the existence of
any 'real' undiscovered cat. The modern folklore motif that concerns
us here is the 'escaped wild animal' story. These tales range from small
events (such as tarantulas lurking in Marks & Spencer yucca plants) to
crocodiles and alligators in the sewers of New York. There are numerous tales of out of place animals of every type going native in the host
country; and occasionally some of them even turn out to be true – just
to thicken the plot, I suppose. The press love to add to these stories
and inevitably the idea that the mystery cats are escaped pets or have
been released, soon gains its adherents.

Although all zoos that are consulted in the case of a mystery cat scare
say that their stock is safe, the public is always wary of the alien in
their midst. Remember in the Harrogate case the lady who said: "They
all come from Knaresborough Zoo, you know" (even though the stock
of big cats at the zoo had been checked at least twice during the scare
and found to be satisfactory. This fear of escaped animals can be traced
back into the last century and beyond; and the British public's fear of
the itinerant circus and animal displays that once toured the country.

Modern mystery animal accounts from both the UK and the USA have
featured updates on this theme, varying from the strange vans smell-
ing of animals that are allegedly seen in some areas before a mystery
animal flap, to the notion that there are people who are freeing big
cats – once kept as pets – into the countryside. The 'zoo escapee' is
simply the most static and easily locatable of these tales – particularly
as the travelling circus is nearly gone from British life. [9] [10] [11]

Another source of 'wild-animal consciousness' are the tales written
about life in the days of the British Raj, which often portrayed man-
eating tigers and the like being hunted and shot; and it seems that the
public loves the frisson to be had from the possibility that there just
may be a wild animal stalking around 'out there' ; even if 'out there'
these days is only rural Lancashire. Furthermore, the popularity of the

image of the mystery cat roaming about the countryside, on the fringes of everyday life, strikes a deep note with the whole of humanity – as fear of wild animals is a basic, primeval one. As most people hear of mystery cats via the media, it could be also be argued that no matter how well in terms of facts the media reports a mystery cat case, it is they who have helped create and perpetuate the genre in the first place; and this is why mystery cat sightings have been on the increase over the past twenty-five years. In the Rossendale sightings, two new factors connected with folklore (ancient and modern) emerged. The first, in which Margansa the witch claimed responsibility for the sheep killings and appearance of the panther, harks back to the beliefs of the Middle Ages when it was thought possible that certain people could shape-shift into animals (usually hares) – which itself is probably a memory of the days of imitative magic and the ritual hunt.

Margansa, in trying to re-hash this belief (whether for publicity or not – who knows she might be able to shape-shift!) only re-awakened a rural community's hatred of the unknown. Had she attempted this scam in the wilder parts of Europe, she might well have lost more than her chapel - even in these enlightened days! [12] Shape-shifting occurs in several other modern-day mysteries, amongst them Bigfoot, ghosts and UFO entities; as well as the previously-mentioned Black Dog (but is not found in mystery cat sightings, other than in this isolated case, which could be a point in favour of the cats having some basis in reality.

The other twist in the Rossendale story is the mystery cat's relationship to UFOs. The UFO flap in Rossendale was a real event, whatever the cause, and the local inhabitants, when confronted with another aspect of the unknown (namely a mystery cat) located it in the place where their last mystery occurred – the quarries. It is worth noting also that the locals said the wild lynxes had been roaming the moors for around five years, which could put their origins in the area – real or imagined – back to the time of the Rossendale UFO flap. This is undoubtedly folklore in the making and if studied, could give the folklorist great insight into why and how folklore develops; and perhaps give an explanation for the adherence of a succession of tales to one particular site – in this case, a quarry. Quarries, pits and mines tend to attract legends and folklore all over the world. [13]

It has been suggested that certain regions are 'window' areas through which things like UFOs, Bigfoot and other oddities can manifest; although from where is never stated. There are well-documented cases of several anomalies such as these taking place at the same time, especially in the USA where UFO flaps often go hand-in-hand with out-of-place-animal reports. With the possible exception of the Rossendale accounts, which I think are purely associative, none of the northern mystery cat stories have any other phenomena attached to them.

CHAPTER NINE

FACT OR FICTION?

Leaving aside for the moment phantom cats from other dimensions, misperception and rumour, could there be any factual basis for the existence of real flesh and blood cats, hitherto undiscovered (although not necessarily of a new species) living wild in the north of England? Let's say yes and see what happens.

One thing at least is certain: Most, if not all, the cats that people are seeing cannot be true exotic big cats such as the Black Panther, Cheetah etc. There just isn't enough livestock in the country to feed all the cats supposedly seen. The eating habits of a big cat (such as a Panther) would soon decimate farm stock very quickly if they were really present in the numbers seen. Livestock slaughter on this scale is not occurring, so it is reasonable to rule the Panther, Puma etc out of the hunt.

EDITOR`S NOTE: Panthers and pumas need not prey on large animals. Much of their diet consists of smaller creatures such as rodents and birds. The rabbit population in the North East alone could support a moderate population of big cats. Add to this deer etc and we have more than enough food. As for lack of livestock kills we have reports from Africa of leopards living alongside farms without killing any domestic animals and even walking past flocks of sheep without attacking them. In other areas farm animals are decimated. It seems down to the individual animals and the amount of wild prey.

In the legend of the `Barnburgh Cat`, it was accepted that the mutilating moggy was a 'wood cat' , a reference to a type of wildcat that once lived in our countryside. There is ample evidence of this in the cat-related place names that litter the country – a Cat Stones and Cat Step being within three miles of my home, for instance.

These wildcats, whose real name was *Felis sylvestris* were largely ignored by the populace. They kept themselves to themselves, lived in out-of-the-way places and were inedible; and so unless they did something stupid (like jumping on the backs of unwary knights or killing livestock), they were left to their own devices.

Although the encroachment of civilisation and urbanisation pushed these cats further and further back into the countryside, wildcats were still being recorded in Lincolnshire as late as 1883 and North Yorkshire in 1840. Could it be these cats - or cross-breeds of them –that have survived to the present day and that account for some of the current wave of mystery cat sightings?

In his book *Lost Beasts of Britain* Anthony Dent questions how they could have survived up until 1883 and answers his own question by going on to note the remote nature of their habitats, largely nocturnal habits and the fact that there were many feral cats whose presence masked that of their older ancestors. Dent also notes that survivors of any species of animal are found on the perimeter of human colonisation; and generally this is where the mystery cats are seen: on moorland, woodland and in wild areas. The Chester sightings aside, there are no accounts from the north of someone seeing a mystery cat in an urban setting.

The mystery cats from the north of England appear to be one-offs, seen for a short period of time in one location and then vanishing (and adding to the aura of mystery that surrounds the subject). I can't offer any explanation for this aspect of their behaviour (if they are wildcats, as it is reasonable to assume, they would be seen more often), but elsewhere the story is very different.

Exmoor, which has been the scene of many mystery cat sightings and associated sheep killings over the past twenty years, has both an oral tradition and recorded evidence of some kind of wildcat existing throughout this century up until the start of the current Black Panther scares. A short extract from Hope Bourne's *Living on Exmoor*, given to him by Fred Milton shortly before WW1, amply illustrates this point:

"...It was, he said, about the size of a dog fox. In colour it was grey or tawny grey, marked all over with dark stripes. Its head was huge in comparison with that of an ordinary cat, and its teeth protruded below the lip like fangs. Its tail was thick and blunt and hung in a distinctive curve behind it. The creature seemed tall on the leg, especially in the hind quarters, and it moved with a sort of slouching gait. To a small

boy there was something very frightening in the whole appearance of this remarkable cat." [1]

This account stands up well alongside the witness accounts in the Harrogate case. The Exmoor area is mirrored for height, remoteness etc by the North Yorkshire Moors (the scene of two of our sightings) and not far from the Harrogate one and also the Pennine Moors on which the Rossendale animal was seen. Despite no wildcats of any kind having been found and recorded in this area officially for 150 years, there is no reason why they could not still exist. Animals are frequently discovered in regions where they were once thought to be extinct. Most of the mystery cats seen don't fit the textbook description of a wildcat – many being black, too big or having stripes and so on; but there could be an answer for this. The cats could be cross-breeds between wildcats and feral cats or, indeed, any variation thereof.

There is now conclusive proof that this type of cross-breeding does go on, in Scotland at least. In 1983, an animal was shot near the small Scottish village of Kellas House. It was 42 inches long and had a shiny, black coat, flecked with long white hairs, a squat head and large canines. A similar cat was caught thirty miles away from Dallas by a game-keeper in 1984 and this one was black, also with a long tail. The Kellas Cat, as it became known, was subsequently stuffed and mounted and sent to various establishments for identification. Naturalist Di Francis was sure that it was an entirely new species of wildcat; although she was still of the opinion that a larger, unknown species was still at large. For a more detailed discussion of the Kellas Cat and its friends, please see Fortean Times No. 45 and the April and May 1986 issue of *The Unknown*.

Di Francis was wrong and the Kellas Cat was later identified by a zoologist as a melanistic form of the indigenous wildcat, and later genetic analysis identified is as a complex introgressive hybrid of the Scottish wild cat, and feral domestic cats. These findings were backed up by the Natural History Museum report. It follows from this that if wildcats can breed black varieties occasionally, then they should be able to produce all of the many types of coloration that people have seen on mystery cats – especially if they are mating with feral or domestic cats. Early in 1985, a BBC TV *Tomorrow's World* special reported on the capture of another Scottish cat; and from blood samples determined that it was a hybrid, a cross between a wildcat and a domestic cat. Both of the previous kinds of 'new' cat could well account for some of the mystery cats seen elsewhere in the British Isles; although these are too small to account for the sightings of larger creatures. One more factor that points in the direction of the wildcat or its variations being the culprit is this: according to Corbett & Southern's *Handbook of British Mammals*, wildcats are not indigenous to Ireland and I have come across no mystery cat sightings from Ireland (Fort does note a spate of unexplained animal killings, however), which should have proportionally as many as anywhere else – if not more considering the Irish penchant for legends. Black Dog legends, however, are prevalent in Ireland. [2] [3]

EDITOR'S NOTE: Alien big cats have been seen many times in Ireland. In one example prior to the publication of *Catflaps!* a lynx was seen crossing the road in front of car in Ballyourney county Cork in 1980. However, these sightings were not widely reported.

As for the larger cats, variations of which the Rossendale and Nottingham creatures seem to portray, they could possibly be an undiscovered cat such as that which Di Francis is searching for; and indeed according to her book Cat Country, has found. As none have yet been caught, it must be pointed out that it is equally possible that they and, yes, even all the others too, could misperceptions of large dogs or cats, which is where this chapter started.

This factor cannot be ruled out. Despite many witnesses being found in professions who should know better (farmers, policemen etc), I have found from my work as a UFO investigator that even the most sane and credible witness can easily misperceive and misinterpret a stimulus. Look at it this way: do you know the difference between a large feral tom cat, a lynx and a panther (black or otherwise – black panthers are only melanistic leopards)? Or can you positively identify a Great Dane in fading light at fifty yards as it disappears into a bush, particularly when you know that a lion is loose in the area? It's not easy.

Most people have very little idea about animal identification and it is all too easy (considering the amount of coverage the newspapers have given to mystery cats) to 'see' something that isn't there in the first place. A rumour soon starts in an area and bingo: 'Villagers in Black Panther Scare' screams the headlines in the Daily Nerd. The 'flap' mechanism works in the same way whether it is mystery cats, UFOs or whatever; as long as there is a stimulus in the first place and a body of popular knowledge to attach to it. Some of this really belongs in the legend chapter, but even the name Black Panther has a ring to it. At least two major criminals in recent years have been titled thus and the name seems to have a grip on the public's imagination, cropping up time and time again.

Personally (and until one of these creatures is captured in England it must be a personal view), I think that the Harrogate Cat, at least, was a wildcat or wildcat cross – and one of many that people are seeing and calling mystery cats, phantom felines or whatever. Perhaps they have always lived in the areas that they are seen in; or perhaps they, like so many other species of wildlife, are spreading from other areas. The Scottish cats make all of this a very real possibility and an intriguing speculation. What will happen to them if they do exist is another matter altogether.

NOTES AND REFERENCES

CHAPTER 1:

1.   *Yorkshire Evening Post*, 31 October 1985.
2.   *Daily Express*, October 1985.
3.   Harrogate Panther ASSAP file. Witness statement.
4.   As above.
5.   As above.
6.   As above. Letter.
7.   *Harrogate Advertiser*, 1 October 1985.
8.   Conversation with Mr Matthews.
9.   Letter in ASSAP file.
10.   As above.
11.   As above.
12.   Conversation with Mrs Cooper.
13.   Letter in ASSAP file.

CHAPTER 2:

1.   *Daily Express*, 16 August 1984.
2.   *Rossendale Free Press*, 8 August 1984.
3.   *Halifax Evening Courier*, 16 August 1984.
4.   *Halifax Evening Courier*, 17 August 1984. Letter on file.
5.   *Daily Express*, 16 August 1984. Conversations with locals. Letter from D. Clarke.
6.   *Pennine UFO Mystery*, Jenny Randles, Granada, 1983.

CHAPTER 3:

1.   *Nottingham Evening Post*, 29 July 1976.
2.   N.E.P., 30 July 1976.
3.   N.E.P., 31 July 1976.
4.   N.E.P., 4 August 1976.
5.   N.E.P., 2 August 1976.
6.   N.E.P., 3 August 1976.
7.   N.E.P., 5 August 1976.
8.   N.E.P., 6 August 1976.

CHAPTER 4:

1. *Yorkshire Evening Post*, 10 August 1976.
2. Y.E.P., 11 August 1976.
3. Y.E.P., 13, 14 and 17 February 1975.

CHAPTER 5:

1. *Scunthorpe Evening Telegraph*, 21 September 1976.

CHAPTER 6:

1. *Sunday Express*, 8 June 1986.
2. *Hartlepool Mail*, 4 August 1986.
3. H.M., 15 September 1986.
4. H.M., 24 September 1986.
5. H,M., 30 October 1986.
6. *Yorkshire Evening Post*, 7 November 1986.
7. H.M., 13 November 1986.

CHAPTER 7:

1. Whitby newspaper clipping (unknown and undated) 1981.
2. *Sunday Express*, 8 November 1981.
3. *Derbyshire Evening Telegraph*, 8 February 1983.
4. *Alien Animals*, Janet & Colin Bord, Granada, 1980.
5. Northern Earth Mysteries Group newsletter.

CHAPTER 8:

1. *Ghost Hunter's Road Book*, John Harris, Muller, 1968.
2. Pamphlet entitled *The Cat & Man*, Sheffield Library.
3. Northern Earth Mysteries Group newsletter.
4. Books of Charles Fort.
5. *Cat Country*, Di Francis, Daniel & Charles, 1983..
6. *Alien Animals*, Janet & Colin Bord, Granada, 1980.
7. *Cat Country*, Di Francis, Daniel & Charles, 1983.
8. *The Black Dog*, Ethel Rudkin, Folklore, Vol. 49.
9. ASSAP file.
10. Articles in *Fortean Times, The Unknown* etc.

11. *Creatures of the Outer Edge*, Jerome Clark & Loren Coleman, Warner, 1978.
12. Clippings as above. Letter to the author.
13. *Pennine UFO Mystery*, Jenny Randles, Granada, 1983.

CHAPTER 9:

1. *Lost Beasts of Britain*, Anthony Dent, Harrap, 1974.
2. *Fortean Times*, various issues.
   Articles by Mike Goss, *The Unknown*, April & May 1986.

APPENDIX

THE CASE OF THE BRITISH THYLACINE

by Richard Freeman

The following article by Richard Freeman first appeared in issue nine-teen of Animals & Men, *the journal of The Centre for Fortean Zoology. It is included because it provides an interesting new slant on the case of the `Girt Dog of Ennerdale` discussed by Andy Roberts in Chapter Eight.*

In the spring of 1810, a bizarre series of livestock killings began. Over the next six months, a mystery predator cut a bloody swathe through Cumberland. This creature was never identified, but became known as the `Girt Dog of Ennerdale.`

Though often quoted, this chapter In British animal mysteries is one of the most cryptic and obscure. On re-reading the tales recently, I found a strange thread that no-one (to my knowledge) has picked up on be-fore. the saga of the `Girt Dog` may be even odder than anyone has ever realised; and the 'Dog' itself may be a doubly Fortean beast.

The tale began when the corpse of a half-eaten ewe was discovered on the fells above Ennerdale Water. the victim was soon followed by oth-ers, as the culprit killed every night. Farmers and shepherds patrolled the hills, but the creature remained unseen. Such was tile quantity and ferocity of the attacks; that natural predators, like foxes were dis-counted. As local farmers became worried; posses of men and dogs scoured the area, but the beast evaded them. It never attacked the same flock on consecutive nights.

Its uncanny elusiveness caused superstitious ramblings among the vil-lagers. More fuel was added to this growing fire; when the beast began to show some disturbing eating habits. Many carcasses were left

mostly uneaten, but the blood had been drained from their wounds, as a vampire would do.

Finally, someone caught a glimpse of the creature. A shepherd watching his flock at dawn saw the killer, but its description brought even more confusion. It was like a tawny-coloured dog, with dark, tiger stripes. Quite unlike anything he had ever seen before.

the Dalesfolk argued over the identity of this strange beast; as to whether it was a wolf, or a lion, or a tiger? Some even believed it to be a supernatural entity, touting its love of blood as 'proof'. Around this time the name 'Girt Dog' was coined. Another queer attribute of the 'Girt Dog' was its effect on normal dogs.

Fell sheepdogs would cower in its proximity, and refuse to follow its spoor. More proof of its diabolical nature, whispered the locals. Hunting dogs were brought in to replace the sheepdogs and a pack was collected to hunt down the killer. After days of hunting, the pack finally tracked down the 'Girt Dog' and forced it to break cover. It tried to run, but the hounds soon caught up with it. the 'Girt Dog' turned on its pursuers with unbelievable savagery, killing several hounds swiftly. The rest at the pack scattered in terror and the monster escaped. Obviously no normal dog could have caused such a bloody rout.

The farmers changed tactics and littered the hillsides with poisoned sheep cadavers. The 'Girt Dog', however, disdained carrion, preferring to rend and slay amidst the living flocks. As the bodycount rose, rewards were offered for anyone who could end this reign of terror.

Once a group of armed men had the beast encircled. The creature charged at one of the men, who lost his nerve and threw himself aside.

Unfortunately, an elderly man, Jack Wilson, who was also quite deaf, was collecting firewood close by. The 'Girt Dog' ran straight through his legs and bowled him over. Jack swore that it was more like a girt lion than a girt dog.

Professional huntsmen were called in, but had no more luck. The 'Girt Dog' led many on a wild goose chase. Up to 100 mounted men with packs of dogs failed to catch it. Finally, on September 13th 1810, the 'Girt Dog' was surrounded and shot. Incredibly it escaped, despite Its wound and ran towards the River Enen. Here it was found cooling its injury and ran once more to Eskat Wood, where it made its last stand. Flushed tram cover and mortally wounded; the huntsmen's dogs closed in and tore it to shreds.

What little was left at the bizarre predator was sent to Keswick Museum, and mounted as a specimen. Sadly, Keswick Museum closed in 1876 and no record was kept of what happened to the exhibits. So ends this weird tale. What are we to make of it? Well, we have some intriguing clues.
The 'Girt Dog' displayed some characteristics which were very unlike any dog. All the witnesses described it as being striped. There are no striped dogs; but this animal must have sufficiently resembled a dog to have been given the name 'Girt Dog`. The animal drank its victim's blood, while often leaving the flesh untouched. All canids eat the meat at their prey. It terrified ordinary dogs, and easily killed hunting dogs, even when outnumbered.

Only one animal could account for these descriptions -- the Thylacine. the striped coat and blood-drinking behaviour at the marsupial wall is well-known. Tasmanian hunter described how it could bite through a dog's skull with ease and Sir Richard Owen described it as *"the most fell beast ol prey"*. This hypothesis may seem fantastic at first, but let us examine some facts.

The thylacine did not suffer from serious persecution until the 1860s. In 1810, it was still a common animal, in Tasmania, where many were kept in captivity. there were no laws governing zoos at the time and although there were only a few sedentary zoos in Britain in the 1800's; there were many travelling zoos. These appalling institutions consisted of caged animals being carted around Britain by horse- drawn carriage.

This must have been a terrible ordeal for both the exhibits and the horses. The best known of these was the infamous Wombwell's travelling Menagerie. As well as the stock-in-trade such as bears, lions, tigers and monkeys; Wombwell's also exhibited rarer animals, such as snow leopards. It is even thought that they possessed a gorilla, without even knowing it! Apparently mis-labelled as a chimp, it would have been the first gorilla in Britain (gorillas were as unknown as yetis until tile 1840's). Zoological accuracy was not a high priority in these establishments.

I refer readers to Clinton Keeling's article "The British Nandi Bear" in issue six of "Animals and Men"). Therefore, it is not out of the question, that a travelling zoo had thylacines in its collection, and that one of them had escaped in the Lake District in 1810. Remember there was no television or radio then. Many people were illiterate, especially in the countryside. Most people know nothing of natural history, outside of their own country, hence the confusion the 'Girt Dog' caused.

Enquiries at the new Keswick Museum drew a blank, as did those at other Lake District Museums, Libraries and Historic Societies. No records of the whereabouts of the stuffed specimens were kept. One hopes that the museum`s stock was sold on, rather than just thrown away. Very little of the 'Girt Dog' would remain now; but it isn't beyond all hope that somewhere, in some dusty basement or attic is a skull labelled `wolf` or `dog`, which has too many incisors and opens far too wide to be either species.

A stuffed specimen of Thylacine displayed in the Kendal Museum, Lake District, the inscription reads as follows:-

"Tasmanian Wolf or Thylacine Thylacines cynocephalus

This is a marsupial (pouched mammal) bearing a striking resemblance, through ' converging evolution' to the dogs and wolves among the placental mammals. Like them it is, or was, a flesh-eater.

Already extinct on the Australian mainland at the time of the first European settlers, it suffered a drastic decline in its Tasmanin refuge since 1910, due to disease and persecution by sheep farmers.

Sightings of the animal have been reported from remote mountain areas, but these have not been confirmed. It is possibly extinct.

Cased by H. Murray and Son, Carnforth"

ANDY ROBERTS

Born: 4/3/56
Occupation: Hostel Manager/Freelance writer
Books: *Catflaps: Anomalous Big Cats in the North, Brigantia Books 1986, Phantoms of the Sky (with David Clarke), Robert Hale 1989/90, Earthlights Revelation (contributing author), Blandford 1991, Ghosts & Legends of Yorkshire, Jarrold 1992, Twilight of the Celtic Gods (with David Clarke) Blandford, 1996/97, The UFOs That Never Were (with Jenny Randles & David Clarke), London House, 2000*

In addition Andy has contributed chapters to the following compilations:

UFOs 1947-87, Fortean Tomes, 1987
Phenomenon, Macdonald & Co., 1988
Fortean Studies 3, John Brown Publishing, 1996
Fortean Studies 5, John Brown Publishing 1999

TV & Radio:
Andy has contributed to many local and national TV and radio shows. He worked as a consultant on and also appeared in:
`This Isle Is Full Of Noises`, Everyman, BBC1, Broadcast 1/11/92
and
Down To Earth, Fourwinds for Discovery channel, also shown on Channel 4
Origin Unknown, Granada, Broadcast Jan/Feb 1999
The Haunted Valley, Granada, Broadcast, November 2000

Major Magazine Articles:

Andy edited the seminal UFO magazine, *UFO Brigantia*, for 25 issues and also edits the sporadic scandal-rag *The Armchair UFologist.*

In addition Andy has written for numerous publications including:

The Dalesman,
Exploring the Supernatural,
The Unknown,
Fortean Times,
UFO Times,
MUFON Journal,
Encounters,
Folk Roots,
The Guardian,
Yorkshire Post,
Bradford
Telegraph & Argus

His article, Rocking the Alien, dealing with pop music's fascination with UFOs was the cover feature article for the July 1996 issue of *Fortean Times* and was also printed in the G2 section of *The Guardian.*

Andy currently writes UFO related column for *Fortean Times* and reviews UFO books for *Fortean Times* on a regular basis.

Miscellaneous:

In addition to the above Andy has contributed research material to many authors in the paranormal field including Jenny Randles, Philip Mantle, Janet & Colin Bord, Paul Devereux and Tim Matthews.

Andy has contributed to a wide variety of small circulation UFO journals and was edited 35 issues of the influential journal *UFO Brigantia*. He has also co-edited the British UFO Research Organisation's house journal *UFO Times*. He currently edits *The Armchair Ufologist.*

Andy is also a prolific lecturer, giving talks on a variety of paranormal and UFO phenomena both at a local and national level, including the Fortean Times UnConvention

Other books available from
CFZ PRESS

CFZ PRESS

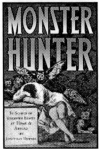

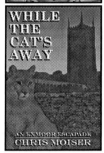

Other books available from
CFZ PRESS

CFZ PRESS

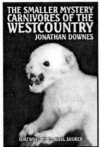

Other books available from
CFZ PRESS

CFZ PRESS

ANIMALS & MEN - Issues 1 - 5 - In the Beginning
Edited by Jonathan Downes - ISBN 0-9512872-6-5

£12.50

At the beginning of the 21st Century monsters still roam the remote, and sometimes not so remote, corners of our planet. It is our job to search for them. The Centre for Fortean Zoology [CFZ] is the only professional, scientific and full-time organisation in the world dedicated to cryptozoology - the study of unknown animals. Since 1992 the CFZ has carried out an unparalleled programme of research and investigation all over the world. We have carried out expeditions to Sumatra (2003 and 2004), Mongolia (2005), Puerto Rico (1998 and 2004), Mexico (1998), Thailand (2000), Florida (1998), Nevada (1999 and 2003), Texas (2003 and 2004), and Illinois (2004). An introductory essay by Jonathan Downes, notes putting each issue into a historical perspective, and a history of the CFZ.

ANIMALS & MEN - Issues 6 - 10 - The Number of the Beast
Edited by Jonathan Downes - ISBN 978-1-905723-06-5

£12.50

At the beginning of the 21st Century monsters still roam the remote, and sometimes not so remote, corners of our planet. It is our job to search for them. The Centre for Fortean Zoology [CFZ] is the only professional, scientific and full-time organisation in the world dedicated to cryptozoology - the study of unknown animals. Since 1992 the CFZ has carried out an unparalleled programme of research and investigation all over the world. We have carried out expeditions to Sumatra (2003 and 2004), Mongolia (2005), Puerto Rico (1998 and 2004), Mexico (1998), Thailand (2000), Florida (1998), Nevada (1999 and 2003), Texas (2003 and 2004), and Illinois (2004). Preface by Mark North and an introductory essay by Jonathan Downes, notes putting each issue into a historical perspective, and a history of the CFZ.

BIG BIRD! Modern Sightings of Flying Monsters

£7.99

Ken Gerhard - ISBN 978-1-905723-08-9

Today, from all over the dusty U.S. / Mexican border come hair-raising stories of modern day encounters with winged monsters of immense size and terrifying appearance. Further field sightings of similar creatures are recorded from all around the globe. The Kongamato of Africa, the Ropen of New Guinea and many others. What lies behind these weird tales? Ken Gerhard is in pole position to find out. A native Texan, he lives in the homeland of the monster some call 'Big Bird'. Cryptozoologist, author, adventurer, and gothic musician Ken is a larger than life character as amazing as the Big Bird itself. Ken's scholarly work is the first of its kind. The research and fieldwork involved are indeed impressive. On the track of the monster, Ken uncovers cases of animal mutilations, attacks on humans and mounting evidence of a stunning zoological discovery ignored by mainstream science. Something incredible awaits us on the broad desert horizon. Keep watching the skies!

STRENGTH THROUGH KOI
They saved Hitler's Koi and other stories

£7.99

Jonathan Downes - ISBN 978-1-905723-04-1

Strength through Koi is a book of short stories - some of them true, some of them less so - by noted cryptozoologist and raconteur Jonathan Downes. Very funny in parts, this book is highly recommended for anyone with even a passing interest in aquaculture.

**CFZ PRESS, MYRTLE COTTAGE,
WOOLFARDISWORTHY BIDEFORD,
NORTH DEVON, EX39 5QR**

Printed in the United Kingdom
by Lightning Source UK Ltd.
124595UK00001B/200/A